THINK LIKE A CEO

49 Tips for Entrepreneurs to Manage your Time, Money, Team and Yourself!

By Alice Hinckley

with Elizabeth McCormick

©2017 by Alice L. Hinckley and Soar 2 Success

Published by Soar 2 Success Publishing

www.soar2successpublishing.com

All rights reserved. Except as permitted as under the U.S Copyright Act of 1976, no part of this publication may be reproduced, distributed, or transmitted in any form or by any means, or stored in a database or retrieval system, without the prior written permission of the authors.

Visit the website at www.yourlightbulbmoments.com

DEDICATED TO:

Passionate Entrepreneurs like YOU,
Who want to harness their resources for higher
productivity and profitability…
one step at a time.

TABLE OF CONTENTS

	Acknowledgments		i
1	Manage Yourself	Tips #1 – 9	8
2	Manage Your Money	Tips #10 - 23	17
3	Manage Your Time	Tips #24 - 34	31
4	Manage Your Team	Tips #35 - 43	42
5	BONUS: Networking	Tips #44 - 48	51
	A Note from Alice		60

A NOTE FROM ALICE

As an entrepreneur for over 20 years as well as consultant to business owners from sole proprietors to executives managing million dollar corporations, I have learned through trial & error, observation, victories and mistakes that mastering the fundamental skills of a CEO will enable your business to thrive.

A Chief Executive Officer has ultimate responsibility for the success and profitability of their business. Whether you are a brand new business owner venturing out in your first endeavor or a seasoned CEO, upgrading your skillset for managing yourself, your money, your time and your team will improve your results.

Key ideas are included in the following pages. Knowledge is helpful. Action is everything. May Your Business Grow as You Think Like a CEO!

Alice L. Hinckley

1 MANAGE YOURSELF

Tip #1: **Take Inventory**

Evaluate where you stand on the main skills for your business.

How are you managing your time? Are you stressed? Is the "to do" list never-ending?

How are you managing your finances? When was the last time you reviewed your profitability?

How are you managing your team? Do you micro-manage or have little idea what they are working on?

How are you managing yourself? Do you own a business or does your business own you?

Download the CEO Mindset Assessment to get a clear picture of where you are today.

www.YourLightbulbMoments.com

Tip #2: **Physical Self Care**

As entrepreneurs, we are all driven to succeed. Of vital importance is taking care of our bodies so we can work at the most optimal level. Establish healthy self-care practices.

Do you drink coffee and soda all day or do you hydrate yourself with at least eight glasses of water?

Do you eat fast food, skip meals altogether or make sure you are prepared with good nutrition for your day?

Do you stay at your desk for hours on end or do you make sure you get fresh air each day?

How do you nurture yourself weekly?

List one thing you can do to improve my self-care:

___

Tip #3: **Your Personal Growth**

"Don't wish it were easier, wish you were better.

Don't wish for less problems, wish for more skills.

Don't wish for less challenges, wish for more wisdom."

--Jim Rohn

Who must you become to surpass all your goals and leave a legacy that inspires others? If you are not learning and growing on a daily basis you are actually moving backward.

What skills or character traits can you develop to enrich your life and your business? Choose a few:

Discipline   Listening Skills   Better Communicator
Speaker   Positive Attitude   Strategic Planning
Marketing   Others:

_____

Tip #4: **Positive Power Machine**

How many hours a day do you spend in your car? Are you always on the phone? Listening to talk radio?

Commit to turning your car into a Positive Power Machine. Turn wasted drive time into a university of self-improvement.

www.Audible.com allows you to download books onto your smart phone or tablet so you can listen anywhere. CD sets are available from your local library to play in your car. There are thousands of free podcasts available online to feed your mind with useful, productive information.

Some suggested personal development experts include Jim Rohn, Earl Nightingale, Wayne Dyer, Anthony Robbins, Brian Tracy, Les Brown, Joel Osteen, John Maxwell, Dave Ramsey.

Tip #5: **Read To Succeed**

So you don't really like to read or think you don't have the time. Consider the compound effect of reading just 15 minutes a day, six days a week, of a business or motivational book.

In just one month you will have invested 360 minutes, or six hours, in your personal and professional development. At the end of a year, you will have poured 72 hours of positive information into your brain.

Where to start? Ask someone you admire either to recommend their favorite book or share with you the last book they read.

Tip #6: **The Power of Momentum**

Do you set goals? How often do you review those goals? Daily/Weekly/Monthly? The most successful people in the world establish goals and review them on a ***daily basis.***

Compelling goals are the key to success. Having a sales or production goal is really just a number. WHY do you want the goal? WHO will you become on the way to reaching the goal?

For example, I want to earn an extra $10,000 this quarter to pay off my car is a practical goal. Add the why to make the goal more impactful. I want to earn $10,000 to pay off my car by the end of the quarter so my spouse can quit their part time job and we can have more family time.

Tip #7: **Visualize Your Results**

A Treasure Map, or Vision Board as they are often called today, is a colorful collage of pictures, affirmations and images that represent your goals and dreams.

Cut out pictures & words from magazines or find images online to print. Create a collage & display where you see it often. For over 20 years I have created an annual Treasure Map with pictures of goals for my business, health, family, spiritual life, relationships and finances. I keep it on my vanity all year long. I also have a 4x6 size Treasure Map in my purse for single goals to remind me even more often.

The visual images will constantly remind your subconscious mind of your goals for the year.

*Tip: **Get them laminated to avoid too much wear & tear.***

Tip #8: **Be Inspired**

When was the last time you watched a movie that truly inspired you? Decide to have a "date night" this week with your family or your love or just yourself.

Pop some popcorn. Make yourself comfy, and watch an inspirational movie. Here are a few recommendations:

The Pursuit of Happyness (Will Smith)

RUDY (Sean Astin)

The Miracle Worker (Anne Bancroft)

Antwone Fisher (Denzel Washington)

The Blind Side (Sandra Bullock)

The Lion King (Disney)

Pay It Forward (Kevin Spacey)

Tip #9: **The Day of Rest**

Even when God created the heavens and the earth, he rested on the seventh day. Recharging is vital to keeping your energy strong for building your business.

Maybe Saturdays or Sundays are your day of rest. Make sure you laugh. Spend time with positive people. Take a walk.

LET GO of work for a day each week. Do not be misled that if you work every day you will have better results. You must rejuvenate your mind and body. So make a decision now.

Circle the day you will truly REST each week.

Sunday   Monday   Tuesday   Wednesday

Thursday   Friday   Saturday

2 MANAGE YOUR MONEY

Tip #10: **Good Financial Records**

Do you have a bookkeeper, CPA or Financial Advisor who can assist you in reviewing the profitability of your business? In order to make sound financial decisions, your books and records must be up to date. Just because you have money in your bank account today does not mean you are operating at an optimal profit level.

If you do not consider yourself to have a financial mindset, hire someone to create your financial statements and advise you on what the numbers mean to your day to day operations.

Consider taking a financial class. Public seminar companies such as SkillPath.com and community colleges offer classes to improve your financial acumen.

Tip #11: **Evaluate Your Expenses**

Are you still paying a monthly fee for a lead generation service? Great, if those leads have been creating income for you. If not, it is time to discontinue. Same goes for any advertising that is not reaping a quantifiable benefit.

Take out your most recent bank and credit card statements. Look at all the recurring expenses. Are they necessary? Are they consistently helping create income? Circle all items to be reviewed for possible reduction or elimination.

Some ideas of what to look for:

How many land lines do you have? Do you still need to pay for a fax line? Can you use one phone line for calls & faxes? Could you just use your mobile phone & secure an online fax account?

Tip #12: **Insurance**

When was the last time you reviewed your insurance coverage and costs? An annual review of coverage and cost could help save you substantially. Sixty days before renewal each year, contact your agent for a review. Also consider getting quotes from a couple of other sources.

Do you have an Umbrella Policy?

Do you have Professional Liability Insurance?

They may not be necessary for your particular business. These questions should be asked of your agent. (And get a 2nd quote too!)

Insurance protects what you have built. Be prudent. Be wise. Right now, set a reminder in your calendar to review annually.

Tip #13: **Pay Yourself First!**

Be certain you are making prudent financial decisions by following the time-tested formula first proposed in 1926 by George S. Clason in *The Richest Man in Babylon*.

First, donate 10% of your income to your church or charity.

Second, move 10% of your income to a separate savings account to Pay Yourself.

Third, set 10% aside to invest in your business for capital equipment, advertising, marketing or personal growth.

Last, operate your business and your life on the remaining 70% of your income.

Embrace this habit now,

irrelevant of how large or small your income.

Financial habits such as this create the life of your dreams.

Tip #14: **Image**

Do you invest the funds in your appearance to look like a CEO?

You don't have to be wearing a three-piece suit.

If you wear logo shirts & pants, make sure everything is pressed and crisp. Invest in good dry cleaning.

Do you have to be dressed in a business suit?

If so, invest in a couple of high quality suits changing your look with the shirts, ties or accessories.

Investing in your appearance so you consistently

portray a professional impression is vital to long term relationship building.

Tip #15: **Quality**

When creating your business cards and promotional materials, invest in a quality designer and printer.

It is so important for every item you share with prospective clients to be professional and reflect you in the best light.

You only have one chance to make that first impression.

Tip #16: **Brand**

Invest in professional headshots for your business cards.

You want to stand out from others, so make sure prospects realize they are doing business with YOU!

You are on their side.

You are professional and operate with the highest level of integrity which creates loyalty.

YOU are the product, so create a brand featuring YOU as the face of your business.

Tip #17: **Be Credit Smart**

Use credit responsibly to build your business. Establishing good credit will help you tremendously when you are ready to expand in the future.

Be smart when using credit. Obtain a credit card where you earn points or miles. As the points accumulate, use them for business travel or to purchase equipment.

Be wise! Pay your credit cards in full each month.

DO NOT purchase extra product inventory or business supplies unless you will be able to utilize them within the 30 day period before your credit card must be paid.

Tip #18: **Join Organizations**

There is power and leverage in belonging to trade associations, a chamber of commerce, networking groups and even social organizations. Annual dues could be expensive so be prudent when committing to any group. Ask yourself these questions:

Are the meetings at a time that will allow me to be involved?

Are other members part of my target market?

Is the education or training they provide such that would help me improve my professional skills?

Just being a member and soliciting the other members for business will not reap the rewards you want. You must get involved so people know you care. In today's world, business is all about building relationships.

Tip #19: **Invest in Your Training**

Budget money quarterly to upgrade your skills. Investing in learning will reap significant rewards in your business when you apply what you learn. You can also throw money away on training if you do not implement ideas into your daily activity. Knowledge is only power when it is turned into action.

Make sure when you attend a training; you choose three action items to complete in your business within the next week. Once you get new ideas or processes started in your business, the results will drive your momentum in performing those tasks.

If you try to do everything suggested from training, you will likely get frustrated and end up doing nothing. Have a strong return on your investment by immediately acting on those three key items.

Tip #20: **Review Income Streams**

Most businesses offer multiple products or services. Which income stream creates the most net income (income after related expenses) for your business? Do you have smaller income streams that require a great deal of resources? If so, does the time and energy invested in the smaller income stream make sense for your overall profitability?

Consider each source of income and how much it ultimately contributes to your bottom line. You may increase income by removing some products or services from your offerings because it will allow you to focus more efforts on higher producing income streams.

Tip #21: **Expert Advisor**

CEOs of billion dollar corporations realize they cannot be experts in every area of business. They may have a marketing background so they hire smart, savvy employees in areas such as operations and finance to build the strongest possible team.

When it comes to managing your money, hire an expert advisor. Ask several people who manage their finances in a way that you respect to refer you to a financial advisor. Interview each of these referrals and establish a game plan to invest in your personal future and the future of your business.

You might want to consider becoming a financially savvy investor by hiring an expert.

Tip #22: **Taxes**

It is crucial for entrepreneurs to have a consistent plan in place to pay their federal, state and local income taxes. Hire a CPA who is a tax expert for small business. Review your financials with them on a quarterly basis. Inquire about tax laws for the year which have either a positive or negative impact on your income tax liability. Planning ahead is essential.

You MUST set the funds aside to pay your taxes or you can create an issue that will steal your time getting it resolved with the government. Most entities pay taxes on a quarterly or monthly basis.

Be prudent. Evaluate your estimated tax liability and make the proper advance payments so you are not surprised by a large tax bill.

Tip #23: **The Law of Sowing & Reaping**

What goes around comes around. That's karma, baby.

We have all heard these sayings. They are another way to express the law of you reap what you sow. Make a conscious choice to pay it forward in life. Smile. Be kind. Get involved in your community. Give back. Have an attitude of gratitude.

How would you describe yourself?

Stingy or Generous?

Friendly or Grumpy?

Thoughtful or Selfish?

Kind or Cross?

Each day we get to choose. Make sure the

Law of Sowing & Reaping is working in your favor.

3 MANAGE YOUR TIME

Tip #24: **Time: Your Most Valuable Resource**

Each day contains exactly 24 hours. No one gets more! The activities you choose to participate in to fill those hours will determine whether your life is mediocre or exceptional.

What one or two activities could you eliminate from your routine and allow yourself more time for enriching life?

What has to go? Circle at least one:

Watching TV ~ Social Media ~ Having Coffee

Extended Phone Conversations ~ Electronic Games

Reading Newspaper/Magazines ~ Unnecessary Errands

Other:_____

Tip #25: **Plan & Prioritize**

Would you attempt to build a house without a set of blueprints? Of course not! So do not expect to have a successful day unless you have created a plan.

When wrapping up your business day, make a list of important tasks for the following day.

Review your list with completing this sentence in mind. Tomorrow will be a success when...

Put a star next to the two or three items from your list that best complete this thought and complete those tasks first.

Tip #26: **Prime Time**

Are you a morning person? Do you need your coffee and a couple of hours to really get going? Do you consider yourself a night owl?

Everyone has a "prime time" during the day when they experience the most energy and clarity.

Schedule your most difficult tasks during your "prime time" this is not the best time for meetings and phone calls.

Also consider the "prime time" of important colleagues and clients. Schedule your most important interactions with them during their "prime time."

Tip #27: **Time Blocking**

Be extra efficient when tackling your high priority activities by time blocking. For example, if you need to make phone calls to new prospects and to follow up with potential clients, set aside two power hours during the day.

When your scheduled power hour arrives, remember you blocked off this time to be most efficient and effective with your phone calls.

Follow some strict rules:

Do not take incoming calls. Do not check email or social media. FOCUS on each phone call so you are fully present even if you end up leaving a message.

Tip #28: **Master Calendar**

Desire more freedom and less mental clutter? Organize your life! Consistency and commitment create the habits you need for ultimate fulfillment in your personal life and success in your business.

Create a master calendar showing blocks of time for those activities. Print out a weekly calendar and choose a different color for each of the following categories. Block out with each color the general timeframes during the week you will commit to each category.

Office Hours ~ Health/Eating & Exercise ~ Family ~ Spiritual/Personal Growth ~ Free Time

Tip #29: **Schedule Life, Not Just Work**

Entrepreneurs tend to be driven individuals. They make sure to schedule and prioritize all work related matters. To lead a rich life, be sure to schedule and make time for family, friends, entertainment, exercise, spirituality and relationships.

Often feel like there is not enough time?

What if you made the decision to get up 15-30 minutes earlier each day?

At first it might be uncomfortable. Once the habit is in place, you have created several extra hours a week to make sure you get your lifestyle activities woven into your normal routine.

Tip #30: **Time Thieves**

Some days you look up at lunch time and feel like you have accomplished nothing on your priority list. While it is smart to have flexibility for important items that arise during your business day, it is also vital to control tasks that "steal" your most precious resource—time.

Actively manage your time for ultimate results. What is the #1 time thief in your business day? Email? Social Media? Phone Calls? Interruptions? Radio or TV? Procrastination?

The next few tips give detailed ideas to help manage the most common time thieves.

Tip #31: **Email**

Set aside a specific time to review your email daily. You may need to do morning, noon and afternoon. Turn off the audio on your computer, phone or tablet that inform you each time an email arrives. It is distracting and takes away from your focus.

One day a week, actively unsubscribe from unnecessary items that constantly fill your inbox.

Set up email rules so that certain email automatically go into specific folders to be reviewed when working on that particular project.

Tip #32: **Social Media**

Let's not kid ourselves. You do not need to check your social media accounts every hour of the day. Yes, it is part of any business marketing strategy today. You must plan for it to be effective. Use a tool like Hoot Suite or Post Planner. Or even hire someone to manage it. You can create and schedule all your posts for the week on each social media platform in an hour.

You will still want to post pictures or make occasional comments during the week. Social media can be a helpful tool. It can also be a constant, time-sucking distraction. Choose to be disciplined and plan your social media marketing.

Limit your social media time, set a timer!

ALICE HINCKLEY

Tip #33: **Interruptions**

Manage how often you are interrupted by setting proper expectations with those around you. Communicate your schedule to others so they understand the best time to connect with you. Post a "Do Not Disturb" sign during those prime times.

Studies show that each time you are interrupted it can take up to ten minutes to refocus. Close your office door. Do not answer unscheduled calls unless it is an emergency.

Allow yourself the quiet focused time necessary to complete the current task at the highest quality level.

FOCUS

Follow **O**ne **C**ourse **U**ntil **S**uccessful

Tip #34: **Profit Producing Activities**

What activities in your business create income? Prospecting? Meeting with Clients? Performing Services? Networking?

It is imperative that you identify the profit producing activities in your business and make sure most of your time is devoted to income producing.

Some projects must be accomplished even though they don't directly produce income in your business. Strongly consider hiring someone else to do those projects for you. In today's world Virtual Assistants (VAs) or outsourcing services are available for hire to complete all types of projects.

Find several VAs—they can all be an expert in a different skill you need to accomplish in your business.

4 MANAGE YOUR TEAM

Tip #35: **Who is Your Team?**

If you have employees, they are definitely a part of your team. Any vendor who provides products or services to help you in your business is part of your team.

Even if you are a sole proprietor, you have a team of people who help your business operate—suppliers, colleagues, referral network.

Identify your team so you can keep them in the loop on your goals, show appreciation for them, learn from them and help them achieve their goals. You are not in this alone!

Tip #36: **Leadership Quotient**

Do you consider yourself a leader? Why or why not?

People want to be around others who are excited and who show interest in them. CEOs have a strong belief in themselves, in their company and in their team and the vision for the future.

Do you have the character traits of a leader that others want to emulate? Do you have the heart of a leader wanting the best for those around you?

What character traits are most important in a leader? When you look at the way you operate on a day to day basis, would you want to follow your own guidance?

Tip #37: **Integrity & Respect**

Integrity means to have sound moral character.

Respect means to esteem a sense of worth

or excellence in a person.

Leading a team requires complete honesty, respect for yourself and all the team members and living with integrity by keeping your word.

Make sure your actions are in alignment with the words you speak.

Operate with integrity and respect.

You will attract business support in your life from people with those same character traits.

Tip #38: **Share & Support Goals**

Having company goals, creating strategic plans, and working towards that vision as a team is essential. Set goals together as a team so everyone feels they were part of deciding what will be accomplished by their hard work.

Remember your team is made up of individuals. Do you know the personal goals of your team members? Why do they work diligently every day? Connect with the personal side of your people and make notes regarding their goals and dreams. Knowing that you care will inspire them. Ask to help celebrate when they reach goals. Make an effort to support them in reaching their goals.

Your team will work harder for your company goals when they know how much you care about them as individuals.

Tip #39: **Gratitude**

How do you show appreciation for loyalty or a job well done? Schedule it! Pick a day each week and first thing in the morning schedule 15 minutes to show gratitude.

Send a handwritten note.

Leave a voicemail showing appreciation.

Recognize their loyalty on a project in front of a group.

Let their spouse or family know with a card, flowers or a gift basket how much you appreciate all the team member contributes to the organization.

Send an authentic personal email with a specific example of how they helped support you.

Invite someone to lunch with you.

Tip #40: **Listening**

Actively listening is a practiced skill. Most CEOs listen respectfully and draw people closer with their rapt attention to the speaker. Do not look at your phone or computer.

Demonstrate your sincere interest in the person speaking by making eye contact, asking questions and not interrupting. People are so often deciding how they plan to respond that they don't fully listen to the comments being made in a conversation.

Be present and attentive.

Tip #41: **Character**

"Watch your thoughts; they become words.

Watch your words; they become actions.

Watch your actions; they become habit.

Watch your habits; they become character.

Watch your character; it becomes your destiny."

--Laozi

Tip #42: **Support & Encouragement**

Team members want to know you support their efforts, encourage creative ideas & initiative and appreciate their diligence.

How do you support your team members?

_____

_____

_____

_____

If you are having a difficult time answering the question, it is time to create a consistent process for showing support and encouragement. What about team member of the week? Let that person share a circumstance in their personal life where the team can provide support and encouragement.

Tip #43: **Expectations**

Setting proper expectations avoids resentment or disappointment in the future. Be clear in your communications regarding deadlines, attitudes, behaviors, quality of work, timeliness and being a team player.

If you have challenges with a team member in any of these areas on a consistent basis, have a face to face candid conversation with them.

Ask questions about why they are not performing at the level you expect. Learn from their answers and determine how to better lead them to the desired results.

BONUS: NETWORK LIKE A CEO

Tip #44: **Authenticity**

Be yourself. Decide which values are most important in your life. Consistently live those values with your words and your actions.

For example, if integrity is important to you in your business then always speak the truth. Not even a little white lie is allowed. You must be honest and open to be considered a person of integrity.

What character traits do you want to authentically shine through you in all of your interactions?

Compassion ~ Intelligence ~ Loyalty ~ Strength

Faithfulness ~ Helpful ~ Generous ~ Genuine

BONUS: NETWORK LIKE A CEO

Tip #45: **Be Prepared**

Networking is a lifestyle. Whenever you leave your house you are encountering new people who may have a need for your product or service. Always have business cards with you as well as other promotional materials relevant to your business.

Have a small notepad or an APP on your smart phone to take notes so you can always gather contact information from someone.

Create your own networking identity so you can quickly share about your business in a few short sentences. Download the Create Your Networking Identity worksheet to streamline this process:

www.yourlightbulbmoments.com/blueprint

BONUS: NETWORK LIKE A CEO

Tip #46: **Networking Events**

The person who ends up with the most business cards is NOT the winner. The person who starts conversations that lead to growing relationships is the ultimate victor.

Your goal is to make a connection with a few key people, not meet everyone in attendance. Introduce yourself to the host and the speaker. Now look for the influencers—they are already engaged in a lively conversation with a few other people. Meet the influencers. Be attentive and interested.

"You can close more business in two months by becoming interested in other people than you can in two years by trying to get people interested in you." -- Dale Carnegie

BONUS: NETWORK LIKE A CEO

Tip #47: **One on One Appointments**

High level networking success is achieved by developing strategic alliances. Once you have made a new contact, set up an appointment to visit one on one about your businesses. The goal is for both of you to have equal time to share about your business. Prepare 4-6 questions in advance to ask and make sure you take notes. Immediately jot down the names of referrals or introductions you may make for them.

Sample Questions:

What sets your product/service apart from your competitors?

What main goal are you working toward in your business?

Is there a specific person you want to meet?

BONUS: NETWORK LIKE A CEO

Tip #48: **Staying Connected**

Have a newsletter?

Always ask permission to add your new contact to the list.

Connect with them on Social Media.

Send a thank you note or email.

Schedule a follow up phone call to thank them for their time.

In networking, the bottom line is to use the golden rule and elevate that a bit. Treat people better than you expect to be treated.

Your business will be energized and thrive in any economy.

ALICE HINCKLEY

BONUS: NETWORK LIKE A CEO

Tip #49: **Referrals**

ASK. ASK. ASK.

One vital step that must be covered when it comes to networks is you must ASK people to help you and ASK how you can help them in their business.

When you realize another person in your network would be a good referral for them, make a professional introduction. Call the referral and let them know you will be giving your new strategic alliance partner their contact information. Share what you have learned about the referral during your business relationship with your new partner.

Be a Connector!

Additional Products & Services by Alice

www.yourlightbulbmoments.com/products

Books:

Women Entrepreneur Extraordinaire

(2013)

Co-Author Alice L. Hinckley CPA

Behind Her Brand: Entrepreneur Edition Volume 4

(2015)

Co-Author Alice Hinckley

Behind Her Brand: Women of Influence

Equipping. Educating. Empowering

(2105)

Compiled by Alice Hinckley

Building Lifetime Loyal Clients:

47 Golden Nuggets for Business Success

(2016)

By Alice Hinckley & Melynda Lilly

Nail it in 90!

For Direct Selling & Network Marketing Professionals

(2016)

By Kim Johnson & Alice Hinckley

eCourses:

Master Networking for Direct Sales Success

(2017)

By Alice Hinckley

Building Lifetime Loyal Clients

(2017)

By Alice Hinckley & Melynda Lilly

Create Your Networking Identity

(2017)

By Alice Hinckley

Think Like a CEO

(2017)

By Alice Hinckley

Nail it in 90! Beyond the Book

(2016)

By Alice Hinckley & Kim Johnson

A NOTE FROM ALICE

Congratulations on absorbing these CEO tips. Now you have the tools to keep you proactive instead of reactive in your daily business life.

Be sure to come back and use this book as a reference when you have a challenge managing one of the areas so crucial to being a successful CEO.

Today is the day! Think & Act Like a CEO!

May your business thrive,

Alice L. Hinckley

www.ingramcontent.com/pod-product-compliance
Lightning Source LLC
Chambersburg PA
CBHW050021230526
45470CB00003B/1069